T0284959
Dior

300 PORTRAIT ILLUSTRATIONS

First edition in April 2024 by Monsa Publications,
Carrer Gravina 43 (08930) Sant Adrià de Besós.
Barcelona (Spain)
T+34 93 381 00 93
www.monsa.com monsa@monsa.com

Editor and Project director Anna Minguet
Art director, layout and cover design
Eva Minguet (Monsa Publications)
Printed in Spain
Page 5, image courtesy of Dennis van Leeuwen.
Page 7, image courtesy of Caroline Andrieu .
Shop online:
www.monsashop.com

Follow us!
Instagram: @monsapublications

ISBN: 978-84-17557-75-1
D.L.: B 4056-2024

monsa

Introducción · INTRO

La ilustración de retratos es un arte fascinante que ha cautivado a artistas y espectadores a lo largo de la historia. En este libro, exploraremos las diversas técnicas, fuentes de inspiración y procesos creativos que dan vida a estas expresiones visuales únicas.

Las técnicas utilizadas en la ilustración de retratos son tan variadas como los propios artistas. Desde el realismo detallado hasta la abstracción expresiva, cada enfoque ofrece una oportunidad para capturar la esencia de un individuo de manera única.

El uso de lápices, acuarelas, óleos, técnicas digitales y otros medios proporciona a los artistas una amplia gama de herramientas para dar vida a sus retratos. La inspiración para la ilustración de retratos puede provenir de diversas fuentes, como la observación directa de la persona, fotografías, emociones, experiencias personales o incluso la imaginación pura. Los retratistas a menudo buscan capturar la personalidad, el estado de ánimo o la historia de sus sujetos a través de sus obras, lo que les lleva a explorar nuevas formas de representación visual.

El proceso creativo de la ilustración de retratos es un viaje emocionante que implica la planificación, la experimentación y la expresión artística. Desde el boceto inicial hasta los toques finales, cada paso del proceso ofrece oportunidades para la exploración y el descubrimiento, lo que permite a los artistas dar vida a sus visiones de una manera única y personal.

En resumen, la ilustración de retratos es un campo vibrante y diverso que ofrece a los artistas la oportunidad de explorar la belleza y la complejidad de la forma humana a través de una variedad de técnicas, fuentes de inspiración y procesos creativos.

Portrait illustration is a fascinating art that has captivated artists and viewers throughout history. In this book, we will explore the various techniques, sources of inspiration, and creative processes that bring these unique visual expressions to life.

The techniques used in portrait illustration are as varied as the artists themselves. From detailed realism to expressive abstraction, each approach offers an opportunity to capture the essence of an individual in a unique way.

The use of pencils, watercolors, oils, digital techniques, and other media provides artists with a wide range of tools to bring their portraits to life. Inspiration for portrait illustration can come from various sources, such as direct observation of the person, photographs, emotions, personal experiences, or even pure imagination. Portrait artists often seek to capture the personality, mood, or story of their subjects through their works, leading them to explore new forms of visual representation.

The creative process of portrait illustration is an exciting journey that involves planning, experimentation, and artistic expression. From the initial sketch to the finishing touches, each step of the process offers opportunities for exploration and discovery, allowing artists to bring their visions to life in a unique and personal way.

In summary, portrait illustration is a vibrant and diverse field that offers artists the opportunity to explore the beauty and complexity of the human form through a variety of techniques, sources of inspiration, and creative processes.

IMAGINARY PORTRAIT

RETRATO IMAGINARIO:

El retrato ilustrado imaginario es una representación visual de una persona. Por lo general, este tipo de retrato se crea a partir de la imaginación del artista y puede incluir características fantásticas, surrealistas o ficticias. Es una forma de expresión artística que permite al artista explorar conceptos de identidad, fantasía y creatividad.

IMAGINARY PORTRAIT:

The imaginary illustrated portrait is a visual representation of a person. Generally, this type of portrait is created from the artist's imagination and may include fantastic, surreal, or fictitious characteristics. It is a form of artistic expression that allows the artist to explore concepts of identity, fantasy, and creativity.

REALISTIC PORTRAIT

RETRATO REALISTA:

El retrato ilustrado realista es una representación visual de una persona que busca capturar con precisión y fidelidad sus rasgos y características. Este tipo de retrato se esfuerza por reflejar la apariencia real de la persona, prestando atención a detalles como la anatomía, la textura de la piel, el color de los ojos, el cabello, entre otros. Los artistas que crean retratos ilustrados realistas suelen utilizar técnicas como el sombreado, el difuminado y el uso cuidadoso del color para lograr un alto grado de semejanza con la persona retratada.

REALISTIC PORTRAIT:

The realistic illustrated portrait is a visual representation of a person that seeks to accurately and faithfully capture their features and characteristics. This type of portrait strives to reflect the real appearance of the person, paying attention to details such as anatomy, skin texture, eye color, hair, among others. Artists who create realistic illustrated portraits often use techniques such as shading, blending, and careful use of color to achieve a high degree of likeness to the person being portrayed.

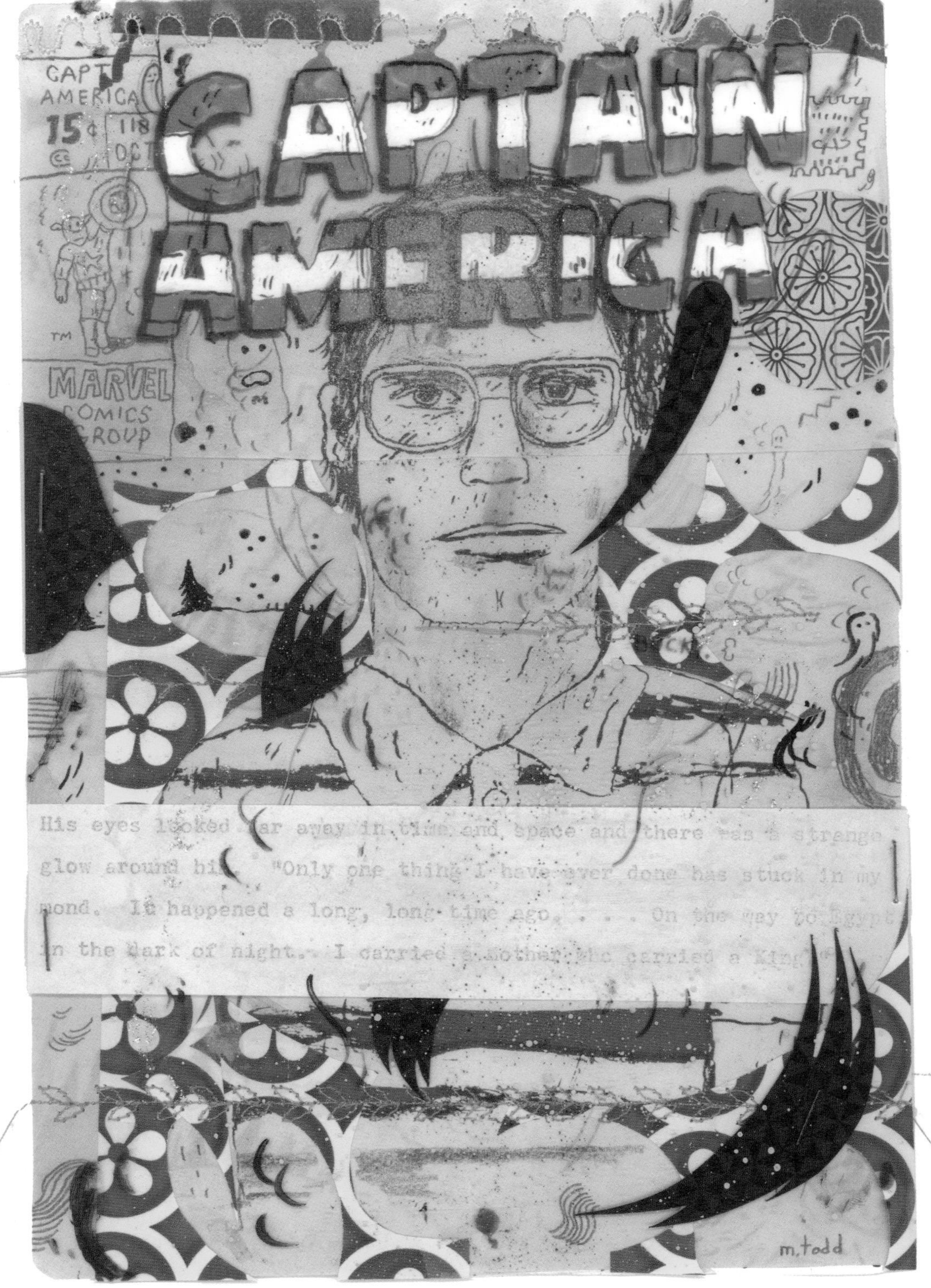

Mark Todd USA www.marktoddart.com

Carried a King. Personal work

Fast Food. Clearasil. Ink, digital

Miranda July. Los Angeles Times. Mixed media

Battle. Personal work. Cel-vinyl on panel

Miranda July. McSweeney's. Ink, digital

Portait. Personal wok. Cel-vinyl on panel

3x3. 3x3 Magazine. Mixed media

Paul Blow UK www.paulblow.com

Music Critic. BBC Music Magazine. Mixed media

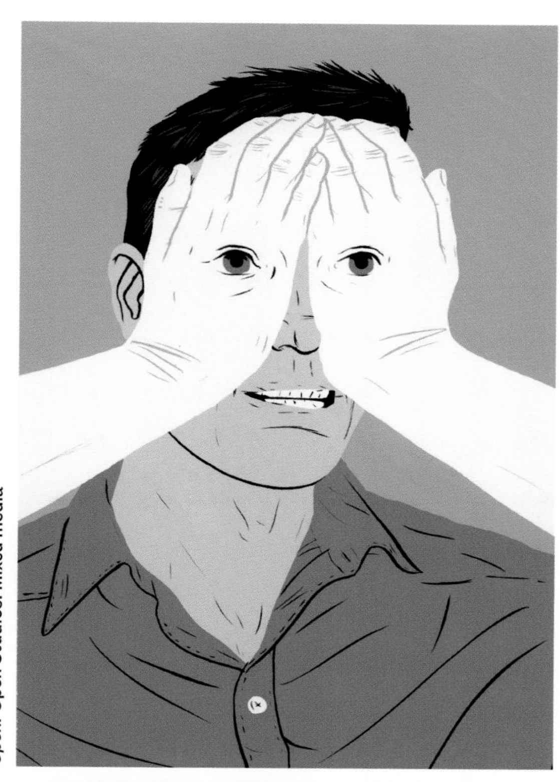

Open. Open Studios. Mixed media

Jack Cashill. The Pitch. Mixed media

The Samaritan. Independent Magazine. Mixed media

Inspirational People. Nonamarmi. Acrylic on Canvas

Jack Teagle UK www.jackteagle.co.uk

God Head. Personal work. Acrylic on Canvas

Devil Head. Personal work. Acrylic on Canvas

Fire and Bone. Personal work. Acrylic on Canvas

Daniel Fishel UK www.o-fishel.com

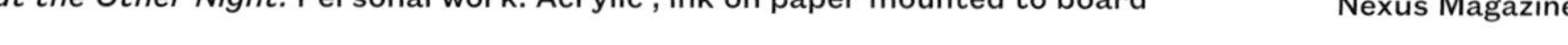

About the Other Night. Personal work. Acrylic , ink on paper mounted to board

Deciphering between whistle blowers with poor information and good information.
Nexus Magazine. Mixed media

Lack of Motivation. Personal work. Mixed media

Mistake Identity. Boston Globe. Mixed media

Happiness. Seattle Met. Mixed media

Marvel Superheroes. Gouche on watercolor paper

Andrew DeGraff USA www.andrewdegraff.com

Marvel Supervillians. Gouche on watercolor paper

Endangerous. Gouache on paper

Viva Freddie. Ink, gouche on watercolor paper

Tilman Faelker Germany www.tilmanfaelker.com

Bee. Personal work. Handdrawing, digital collage

Me and my Polygon. Personal work. Hand drawing, digital collage

Mask Girl. Personal work. Hand drawing, digital collage

Stealth Girl. Personal work. Hand drawing, digital collage

I HAVE BEEN TO THE MOON WITHOUT YOU

I,ve Been to the Moon Without You. Personal work. Hand drawing digital collage

Marcus Oakley UK wwwmarcusoakley.com

Adam. Nieves. Pencil

Joseph. Nieves. Pencil

Xuan. Personal work

Andy. Nieves. Pencil

Clare. Nieves. Pencil

French. Nieves. Pencil

Hayley. Nieves. Pencil

Sarah McNeil New Zeland www.400pencils.com

Awkward Conversation. Real EatsMagazine. Pencil, gouache on paper

The Piper. Once Upon exhibition. Pencil, gouache on paper

Straw Hat. Personal work. Pencil, ink on paper

Tattoo Sweater and the Colours of Everything Inside. Personal work. Pencil, gouache on paper

Branch from the White Forest. Pencil, gouache on paper

Asako Masunouchi Japan www.asako-masunouchi.com

Avril. Mr.Brown & Vue sur la Ville. Felt pen, Photoshop

I'll Write to You Soon. Velvet Morning. Color pencil

Belle Époque. Personal work. Color pencil

It Will Be Found Later. Personal work. Felt pen, Photoshop

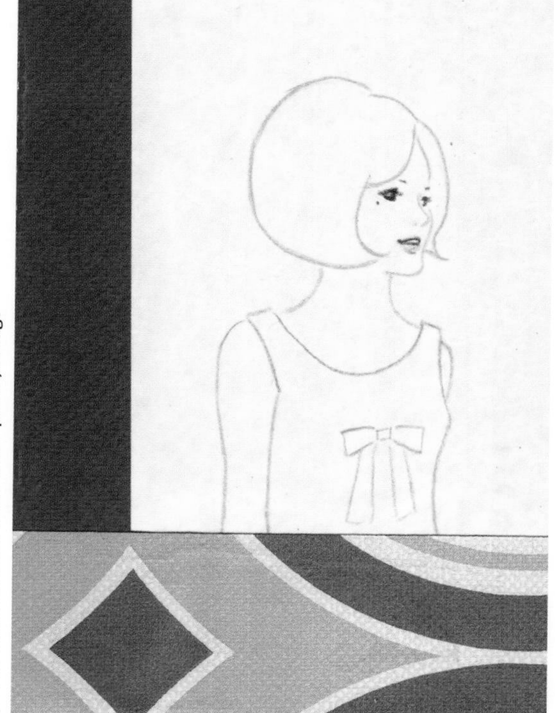

Poupée de Son. Personal work. Color pencil, collage

Fight Flight. La Luz de Jesús Gallery. Ink, graphite

Minions. LA Weekly. Ink, gouache, graphite

Cracked/Tangled. La Luz de Jesús Gallery. Ink, gouache, col-erase

Bryce Wymer USA www.aflatearth.com

The Moby's 02. Personal work. Textured gouache, India ink, digital

The Moby's 01. Personal work. Textured gouache, India ink, digital

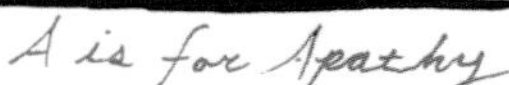
A is for Apathy

A is for Apathy. Personal work. Textured gouache, India ink, digital

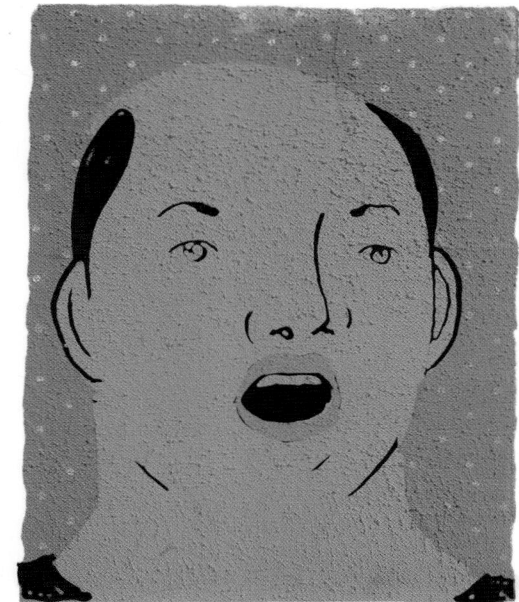
O is for Outrage

O is Outrage. Personal work. Textured gouache, India ink, digital

E is for Envy

E is Envy. Personal work. Textured gouache, India ink, digital

Hellen. Personal work. Gouache, India ink, collage on found object

Ken Garduno USA www.kengarduno.com

We the People. Personal work. Acrylic ink, wash

Bernadette. Personal work. Gouache

Narcissim. Personal work. Acrylic ink, wash

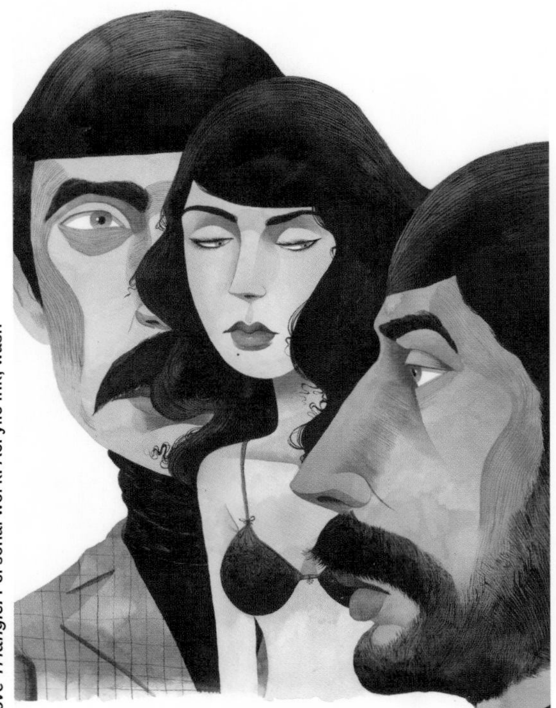

Love Triangle. Personal work. Acrylic ink, wash

Birthday Party. Personal work. Acrylic ink, wash

Russ Mills UK www.byroglyphics.com

Equinopsis. Personal work. Digital composite

Astrophytum. Personal work. Digital composite

Delphinium. Personal work. Digital composite

Gethsemane. Domestic Science. Show at Signal Gallery. Digital composite

Asphyxsia. Personal work. Digital composite

Sandra Haselsteiner Germany www.sandra-haselsiner.de

Confetti Drawing. Personal work. Watercolor, confetti, digital

You are so Beautiful - We are Family. Personal work. Watercolor

You are so Beautiful - Hair. Personal work. Watercolor

Kisses. Schnitt. Marker, felt pen, ink pen, digital

Anna Halarewicz Poland www.annahalarewicz.eu

Pure Red & Black. Personal work. Watercolor, crayon, ink

A Tribute to Alexander McQueen. Personal work. Watercolor, crayon, ink

Pure Red & Black. Personal work. Watercolor, crayon, ink

Pure Red & Black. Personal work. Watercolor, crayon, ink

Pure Red & Black. Personal work. Watercolor, crayon, ink

The death. Lips Magazine

Rainy. Chick Happens Magazine

Gold and Silver. Lips Magazine

True Nature. Personal work

Octopus Lovers. Personal work

Carne Griffiths UK www.carnegriffiths.de

Comfort. Personal work. Ink, tea on watercolor paper

Metamorphosis. Personal work. Ink, tea on watercolor paper

Strenght. Personal work. Ink, tea on watercolor paper

Parassita. Personal work. Ink, tea on watercolor paper

Take Cover. Personal work. Ink, tea on watercolor paper

Anna. Personal work. Japanese woodcut printing

Annette. Personal work. Japanese woodcut printing

Ferhat. Personal work. Japanese woodcut printing

Sanne. Personal work. Japanese woodcut printing

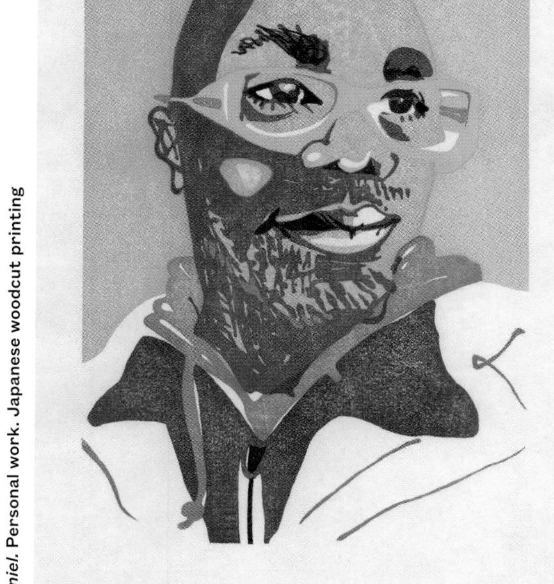

Daniel. Personal work. Japanese woodcut printing

Claudia Carieri Italy www.claudiacarieri.com

Sailor Girl. Poolga. Digital

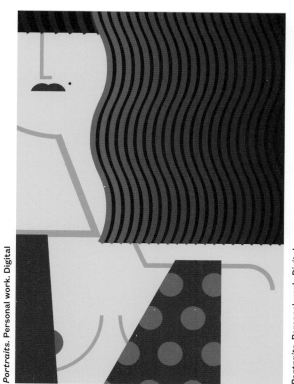

Portraits. Personal work. Digital

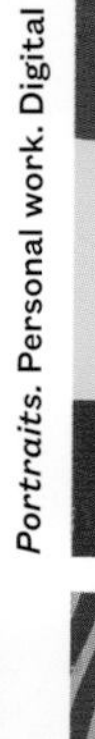

Portraits. Personal work. Digital

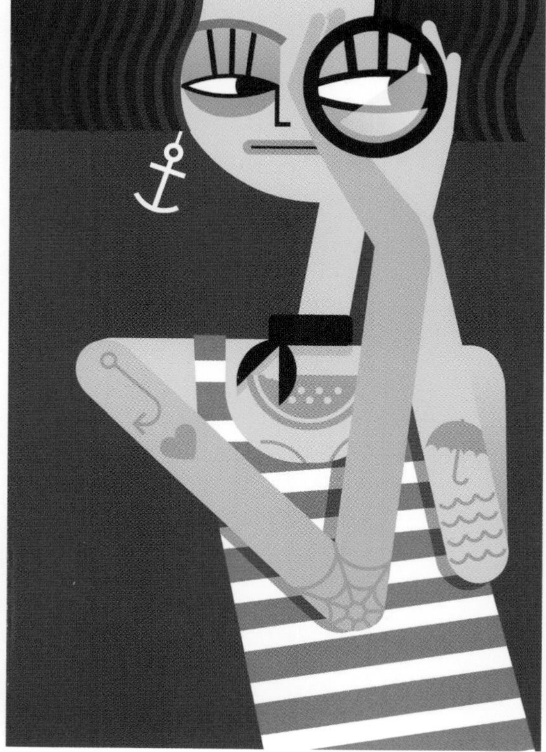

Sailor Girl. Poolga. Digital

Portraits. Personal work. Digital

Begoberlin Japan www.begoberlin.web.fc2.com

Friend's friends 6. Personal work. CG

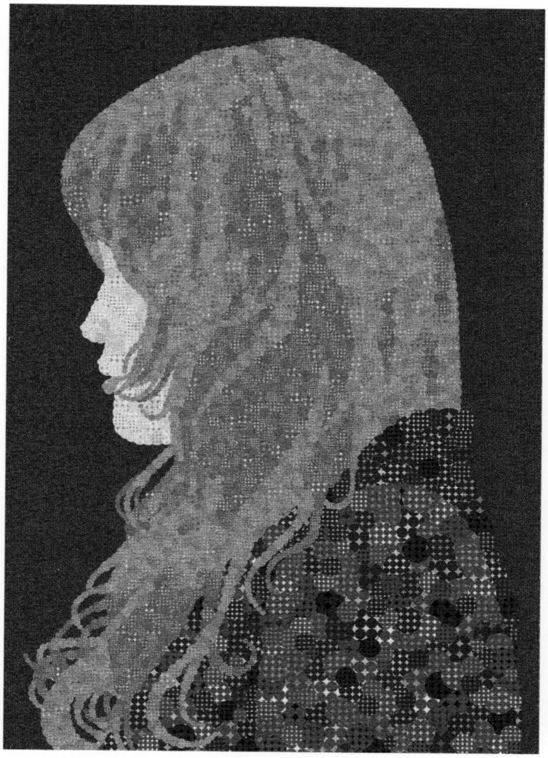

Friend's friends 3. Personal work. CG

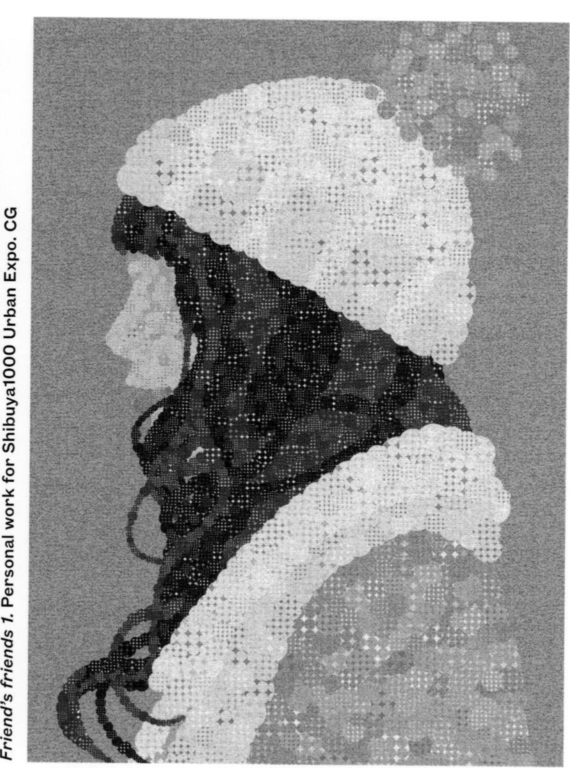

Friend's friends 1. Personal work for Shibuya1000 Urban Expo. CG

Friend's friends 4. Personal work.CG

Friend's friends 5. Personal work. CG

Jordan Grace Owens USA www.jordangrace.com

Ronnie. Illustration for band poster.Acrylic on paper

Seamist. BPersonal work. Acrylic on paint sample

Deep Cowslip. Personal work. Acrylic on paint sample

Lucy. Personal work. Acrylic on paint sample

Lady on Red. Personal work. Acrylic on paint sample

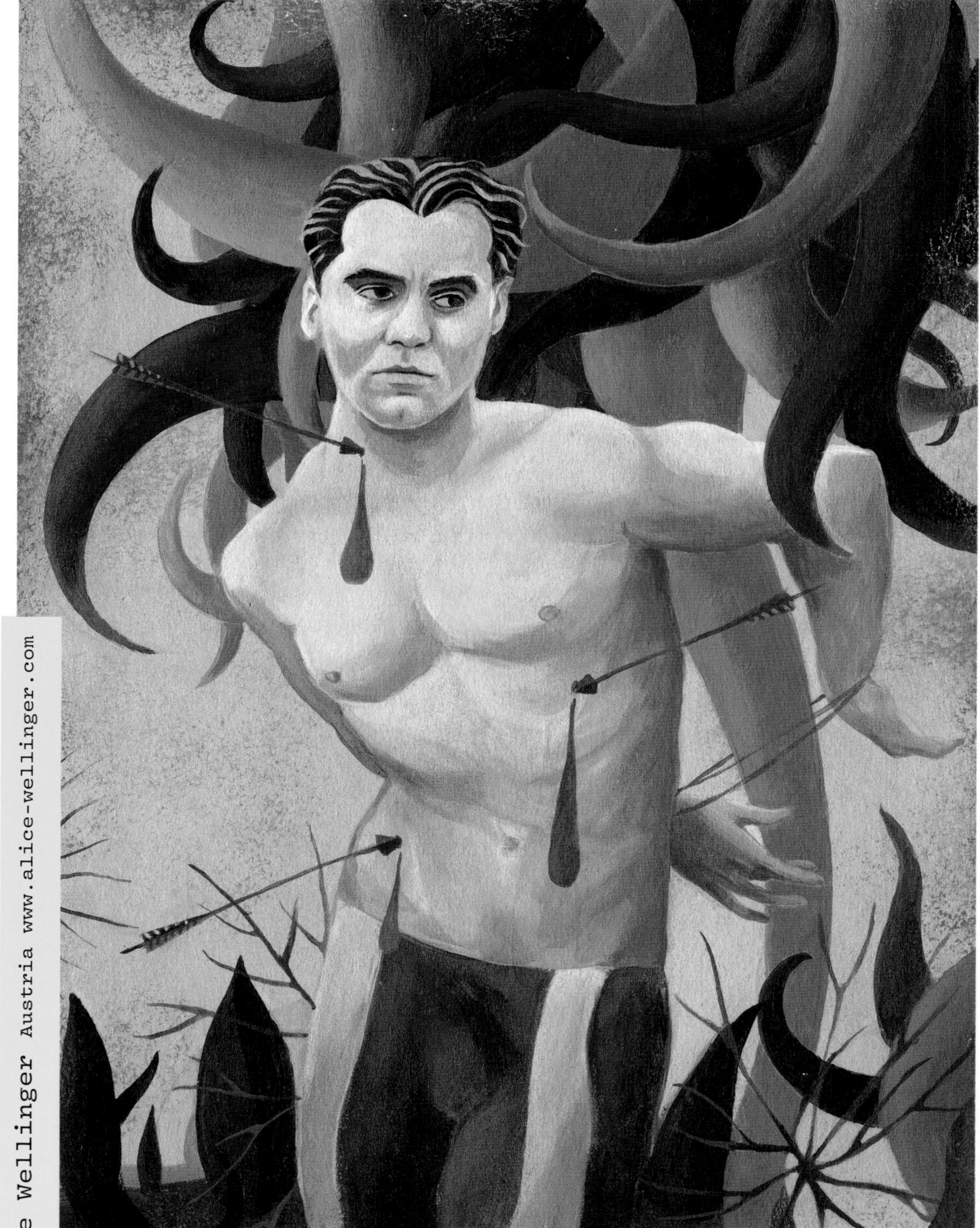

Federico García Lorca. Personal work. Acrylic on cardboard

Alice Wellinger Austria www.alice-wellinger.com

Don't LookBack. Personal work. Acrylic, digital

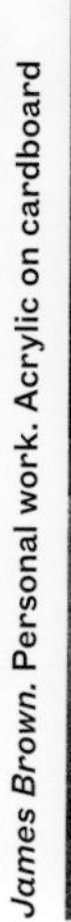

James Brown. Personal work. Acrylic on cardboard

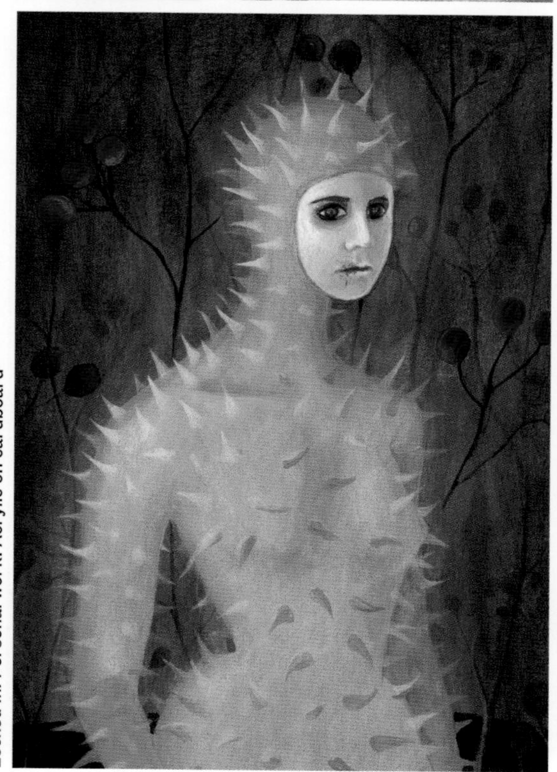

Locked In. Personal work. Acrylic on cardboard

Medizin aus dem Regenwald. Vital Magazim. Acrylic, digital

Aidan Meighan UK www.meighanillustrations.blogspot.com

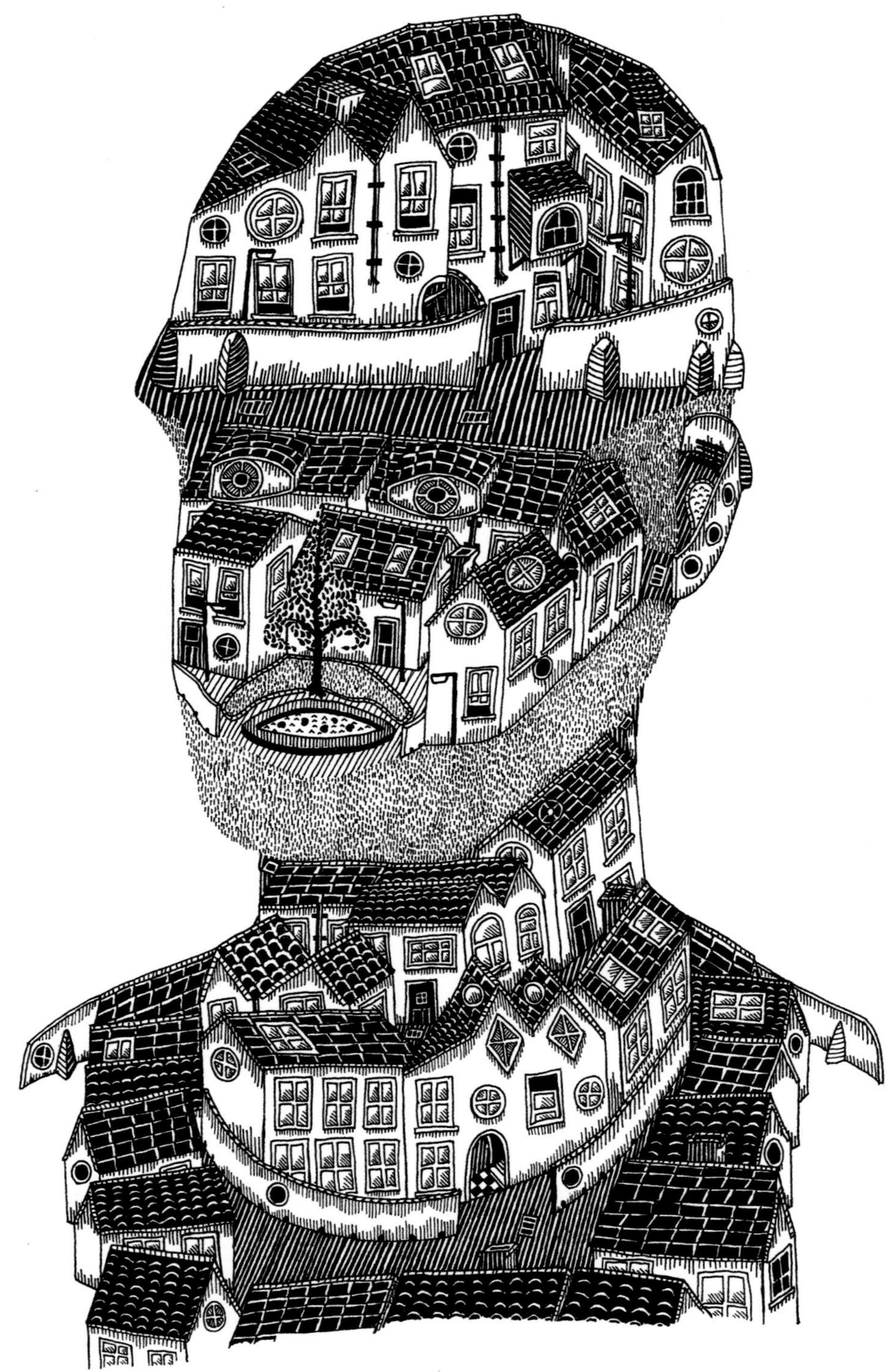

Builder. Personal work. Pen

Farmer. Personal work. Pen

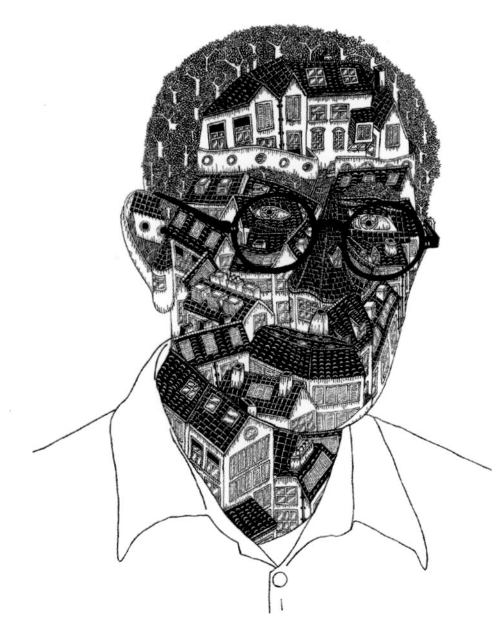

Sir Peter Cook. 75 Peter Show. Pen

Lumberjack. Personal work. Pen

Fisherman. Personal work. Pen

Jessica Singh Austria www.jessicasingh.com

You Stung Me. Personal work. Digital

Long Gone Down. Personal work. Pencil, digital

Rapunzel. Personal work. Ink, watercolor

Sierra. Vital Magazim. Digital

Denise van Leeuwen Netherlands www.denisevanleeuwen.com

Moederschapsideologie. Lof. Pen, pencil on paper, colored in Photoshop

Water. Annabelle. Pen, pencil on paper, colored in Photoshop

Kusetiquette. ELLE NL. Pen, pencil on paper, colored in Photoshop

Pulling Skin. Annabelle. Pen, pencil on paper, colored in Photoshop

Elke Dag Seks. Viva. Pen, pencil on paper, colored in Photoshop

Ant Hayes Australia www.antisant.com

Shirley. Personal work. Digital

Mieko. Personal work. Digital

Lantian. Personal work. Digital

Cory. Personal work. Digital

Misfit. Personal work. Digital

STRIKE A POSE FOR THE CAMERA & SAY CHEEEESSSEE!!!

MICKEY HIDE MINNIE. RASTAMOUSE IS IN THE HOUSE. AND HE AINT LOOKING FOR CHEESE!!

IT SUCKS WHEN YOU DON'T HAVE NO CHEE$E

IM LACTOSE INTOLERANT BIATCH!!

1823

RASTA MOUSE RUNS TINGS !!!

TRY TO MAKE ENDS MEET, YOU'RE A SLAVE TO MONEY THEN YOU DIE

I♥R.M.

MR.FRIVOLOUS.!!

Don't Take the Mickey I'm Lactose Intolerant. Personal work. Felt tip pens

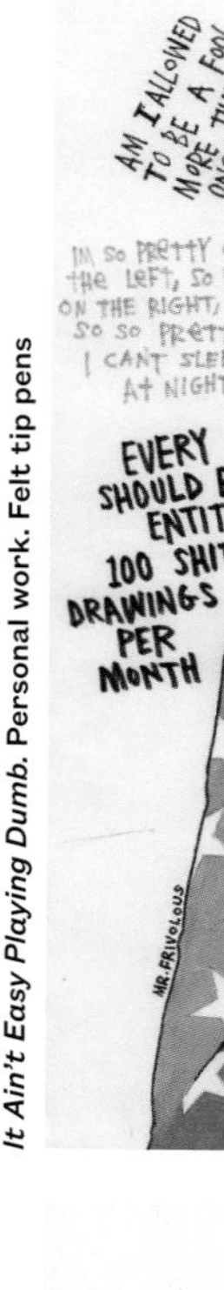

It Ain't Easy Playing Dumb. Personal work. Felt tip pens

See No Evil. Personal work. Felt tip pens

Sometimes Life is Funny Without the HA HA. Personal work. Felt tip pens

Anxiety Always. Personal work. Felt tip pens

Daniel Mackie UK www.danielmackie.com

Don Draper from Mad Men. Personal work. Watercolor

Bjork. Personal work. Watercolor

Chuck Berry .Personal work. Watercolor

Chris Arran UK www.chrisarran.com

Yippee. Personal work. Digital media, paint

Cops. Personal work. Digital media, paint, pencil

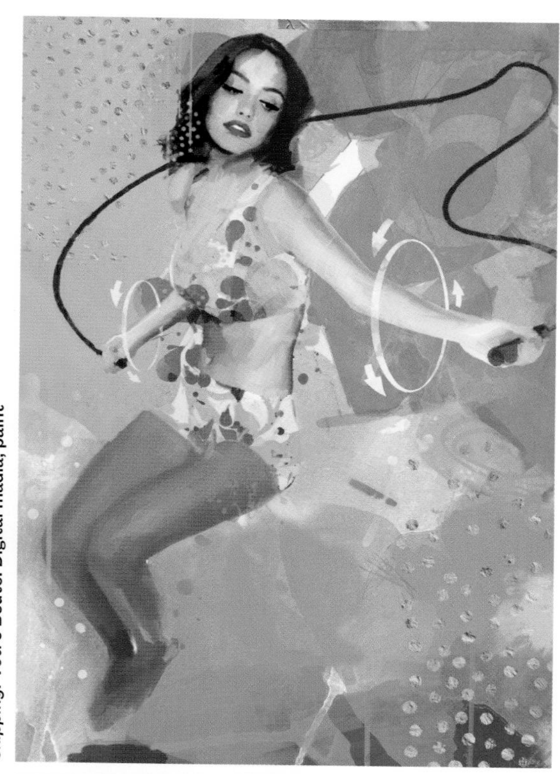

Skipping. Votre Beute. Digital madia, paint

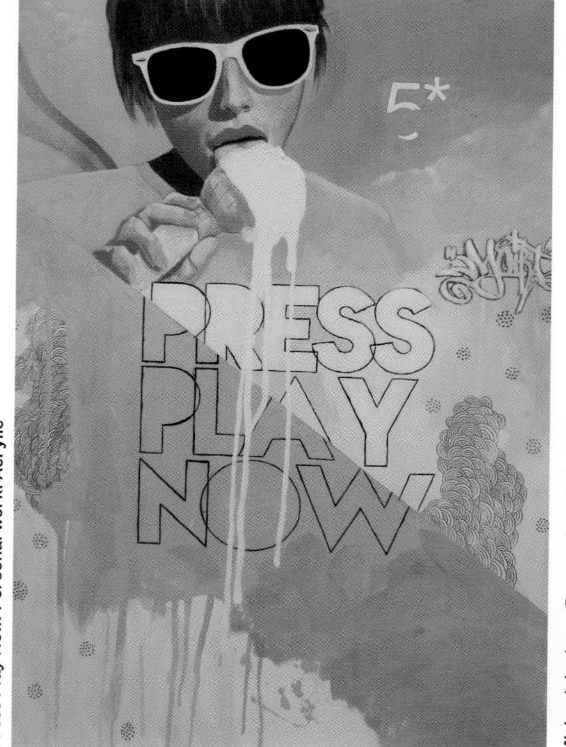

Press Play Now. Personal work. Acrylic

Michael Jackson. Personal work. Acrylic

Hipster. Das Magazin, Tages Anzeiger. Digital

Grego Gilbert-Lodge Switzerland www.gilbert-lodge.com

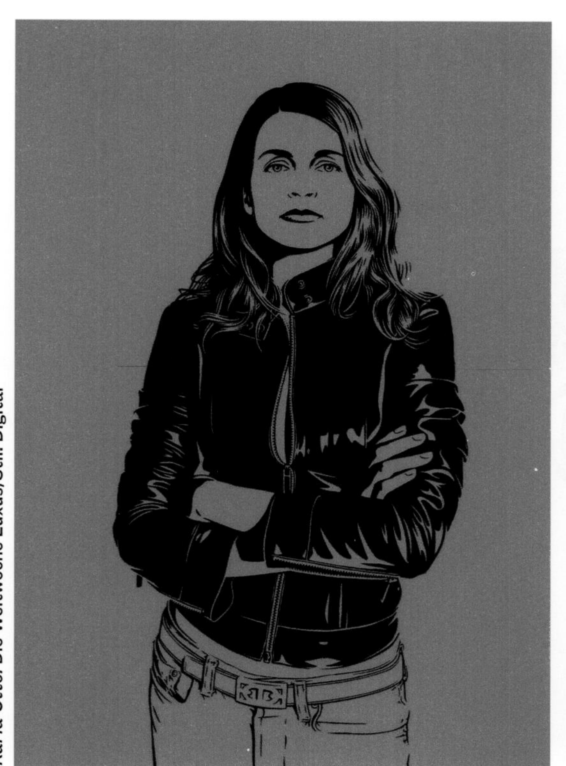

Karla Otto. Die Weltwoche Luxus/Stil. Digital

Fraeulein Braun. Personal work. Silkscreen printbon paper

Graciebird. Personal work. Digital

Diana. Personal work. Silkscreen print on paper

Vivienne. Smart Guide. Ball pen on paper

Terry. Smart Guide. Ball pen on paper

Melancholy. Personal work. Ball pen on paper

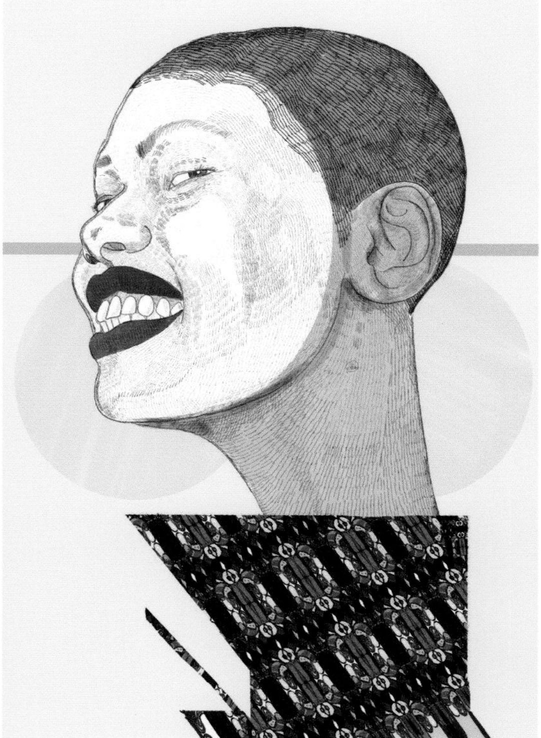

Smile. Personal work. Ball pen, pencil, collage

Untitled. Milk X Magazine. Ball pen, digital

Florian Nicolle aka Neo France www.neo-innov.fr

Allen Iverson. Personal work. Tradigital

Lize. Personal work. Tradigital

Y. Personal work. Tradigital

Iris. Personal work. Tradigital

Jermain Defoe. Personal work. Tradigital

Caroline Andrieu France www.untitled-07.com

Mariacarla & Maryna for Louis Vuitton. Personal work. Pencil

Tati for Marni. Vogue France. Ink

Lea. Personal work. Colored pencil

Barry Falls Ireland www.barryfalls.com

Barack Obama. Spectator

The Arcade Fire. Personal work

Woman With Necklace. Personal work

Paul. Personal work

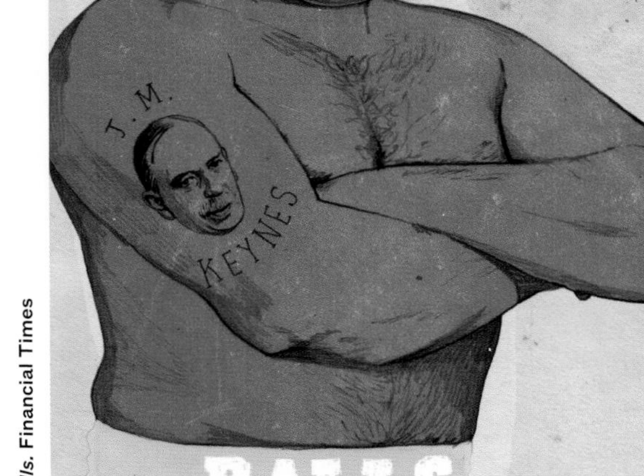

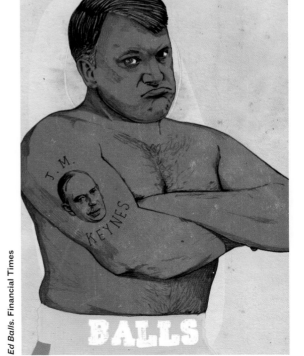

Ed Balls. Financial Times

Jörn Kaspuhl Germany www.kaspuhl.com

Bat For Lashes. Personal work. Ink, Photoshop

R.E.M. Rolling Stone. Ink, Photoshop

Joanna Newsom 2. Rolling Stone. Ink, Photoshop

Phoenix. Magic Magazine Hors Série. Digital

Anne. Personal work. Ink on paper

Serge Gainsbourg. L'integrale Gainsbourg by Gilles Verlant & Loic Picaud, Fetjaine Editions. Ink on paper

Marc Jacobs. Personal work. Ink on paper

Amiral Nelson. Social Club Magazine. Ink on paper

日本へ
愛を込めて
FOR JAPAN
WITH LOVE

Ëlodie France www.elodie-illustrations.net

For Japan with Love. Personal work. Pencil, watercolor, Photoshop

Charlotte. La Marelle Editions. Pencil, Photoshop

Sexy Mor. Personal work. Pencil, watercolor, Photoshop

Poupée Russe. La Marelle Editions. Pencil, watercolor, Photoshop

Rebecca Abell UK www.rebeccaabell.co.uk

Winter. Personal work.

Double Dutch. Personal work.

Afetr the Rain. Personal work.

Matthew Hollings UK www.matthew-hollings.com

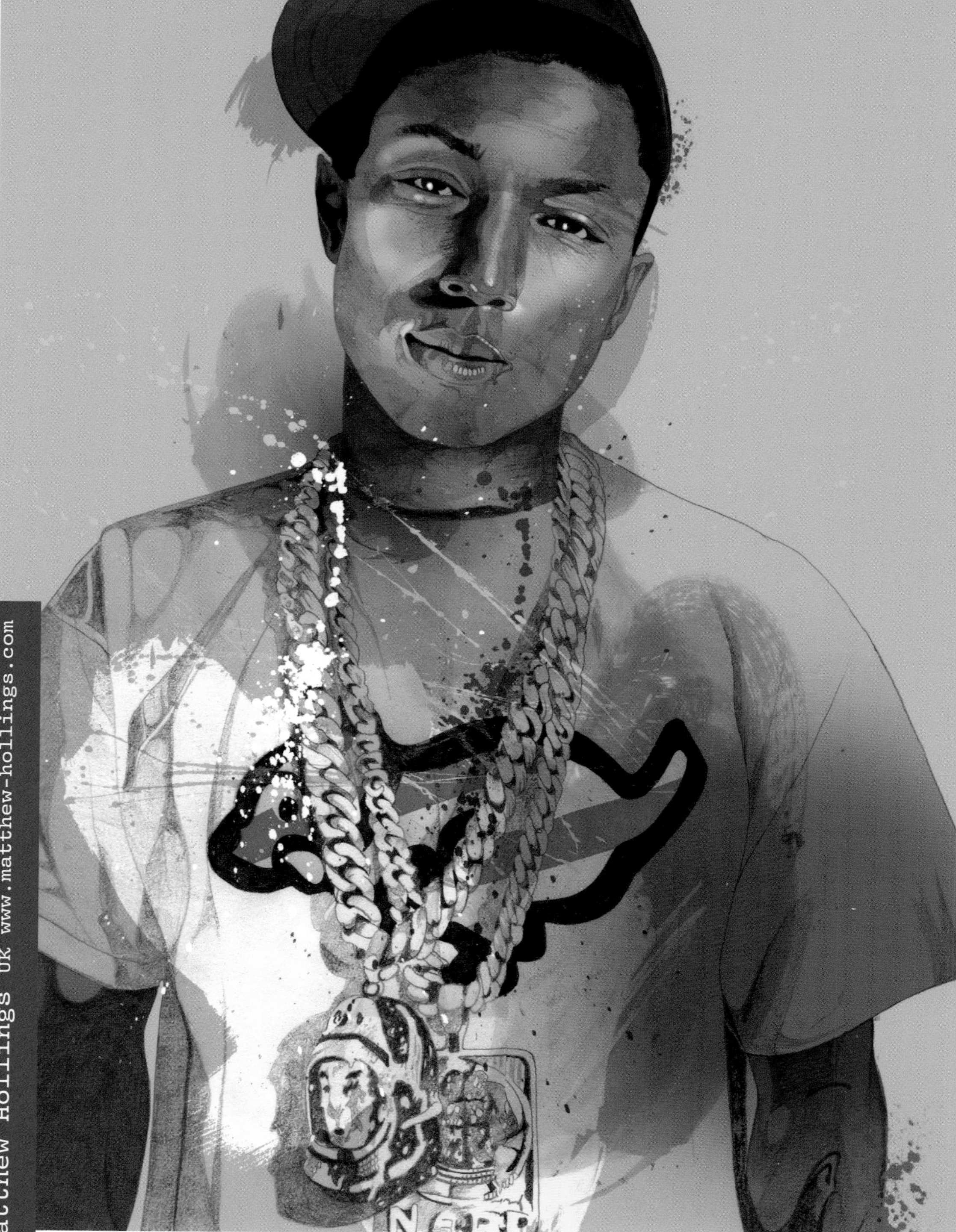

Pharrell Williams. Arise Magazine. Digital

Herbie Hancock. Personal work. Digital

Madonna. Personal work. Digital

Natalie Cole. Rochester International Jazz Festival. Digital

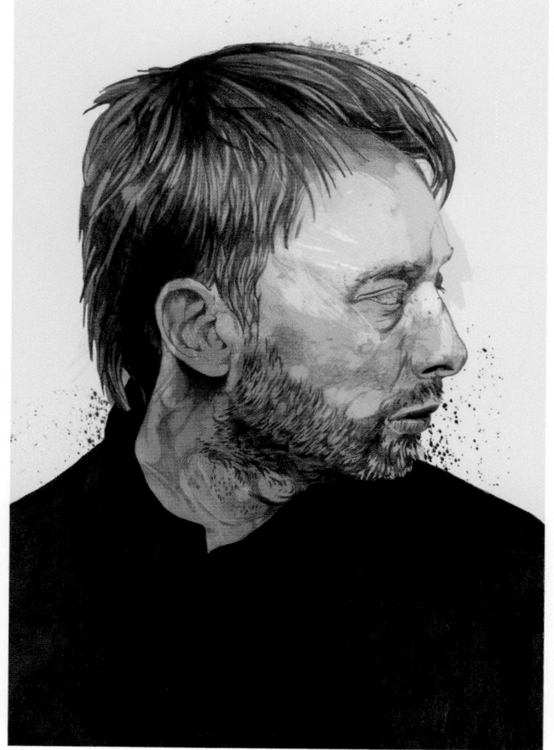

Thom Yorke. Personal work. Digital

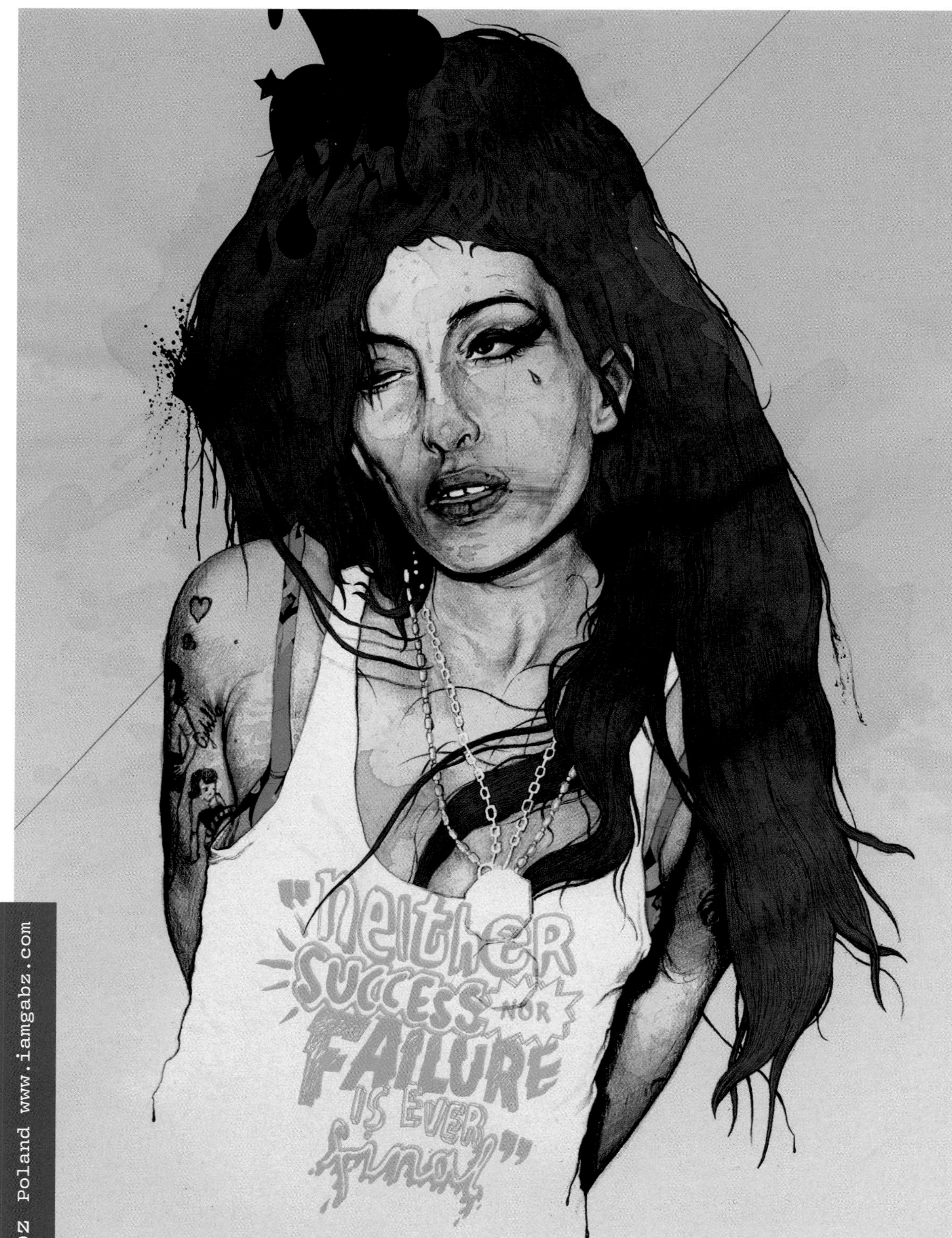

Amy. Personal work. Pencil, Photoshop

Blade Runner. Personal work. Illustration, Photoshop

Death Wish. Personal work. Pencil, Photoshop

Dirty Dozen. Personal work. Pencil, Photoshop

Rena Littleson Australia www.renalittleson.com

Entwined. **Pencil on paper**

Anonymous. Pencil on paper

Undercover. Pencil on paper

Utopia. Pencil on paper

Invisible. Pencil on paper

Ini Neumann Germany www.jmiuminou.com

Requiem. Personal work. Digital print

Alicen. Personal work. Digital print

Zooey. Votre Beute. Digital print

Mieze. Personal work. Digital print

Bianca Heinrichs aka la Robotique Germany www.rbtq.de

Sarah. Piaui#33 magazine. Freehand, Photoshop

Sarah & Malte. Personal work. Freehand, Photoshop

Boys. Personal work. Freehand, Photoshop

Jürgen Grewe Germany www.juergengrewe.com

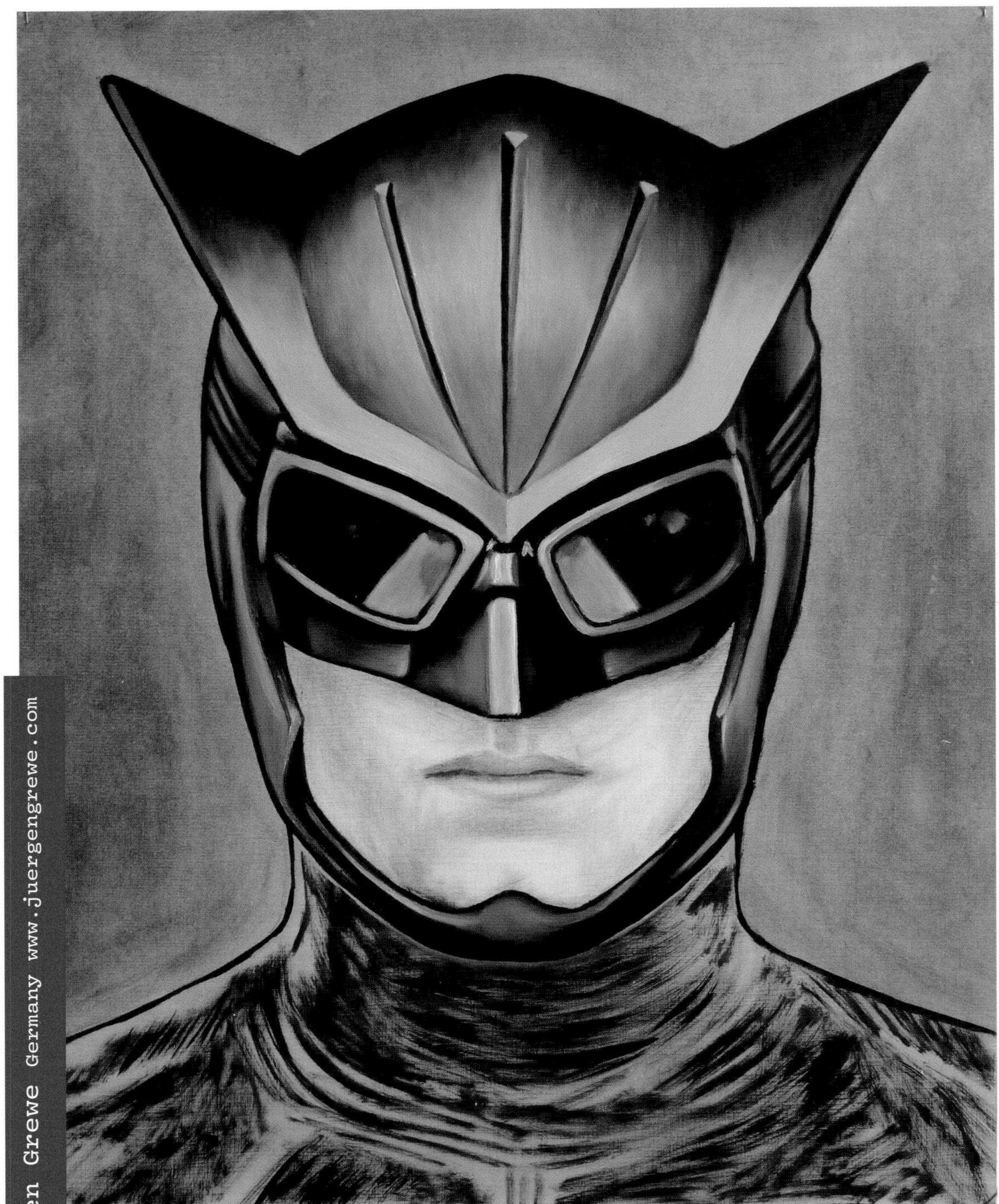

Nightowl. Personal work. Oil on paper

Blond Girl. Personal work. Oil on paper

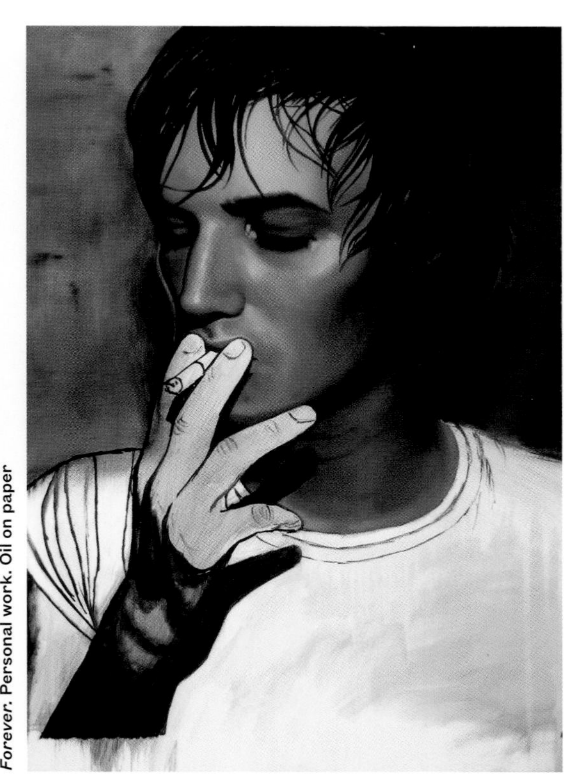

Forever. Personal work. Oil on paper

Tom. Personal work. Oil on paper

Dark Eyes. Personal work. Oil on paper

Kimi Kimoki France www.kimikimoki.blogspot.com

New teenagers of Marseille 1. Personal work. Lead pencil, pencils, Photoshop

***New teenagers of Marseille 2*. Personal work. Lead pencil, pencils, Photoshop**

***No title. Frojo Jewelry*. Lead pencil, pencils, Photoshop**

Patrick McQuade USA www.patrickmcquade.com

Brigitte Bardot. Personal work. Traditional, digital

Conan O'Brien. Royal Flush Magazine. Digital

Jay Leno. Royal Flush Magazine. Digital

Brad Pitt. Royal Flush Magazine. Digital

Hunter S. Thompson. Commission. Traditional, digital

Oh Margot!. Personal work. Pencil, watercolor

Esra Røise Norway www.esraroise.com

Lola. Personal work. Pencil, watercolor, collage

Noone belongs here more than you. Personal work. Pencil, watercolor

Jeanne. Milk magazine. Mixed media

Birgitte. Milk magazine. Mixed media

Adam James Turnbull Australia www.behance.net/search/projects/adamjamesturnbull

Jelly Demon. Ink drawing, watercolor, digital color

Mirror. Ink drawing, digital color

Carpet. Personal work. Ink drawing, digital color

Mirror. Ink drawing, digital color

Carpet. Personal work. Ink drawing, digital color

Matthieu Appriou aka Telmolindo France www.telmolindo.net

Untitled. Exhibition IP_Paris. Pencil, India ink, watercolors

Childhood dream 3. Personal work. Digital drawing, watercolors

Lumi. Personal work. Digital drawing, watercolors

Alex H. Personal work. Digital drawing, watercolors

Jarvis Cocker. Personal work. Acrylic ink, acrylic paint

Cheeky in Check. Tor Press. Acrylic ink

Peter Docherty. Personal work. Acrylic ink, Photoshop

Ree Ree. Personal work. Pencil

Stop Having Fun. Personal work. Acrylic ink, Photoshop

Blade Runner. New Age Media. Ink drawing, digital color

Jelly Demon. Ink drawing, watercolor, digital color

Mirror. Ink drawing, digital color

Carpet. Personal work. Ink drawing, digital color

Cocoroise. Ink drawing, digital color

Mary Wells. Edel Verlag + EMI. Pencil drawing, acrylic color, digital collage

The Black Keys, El Camino. Rolling Stone. Pencil drawing, acrylic color, digital collage

TV on the Radio. Rolling Stone. Pencil drawing, acrylic color, digital collage

Perceptions. Promotional work. Pencil, oil pastel, watercolor, Photoshop

Sir David Attenborough. Personal work. Pencil, mono print, oil pastel, watercolor, Photoshop

Frolicsome Poster. Promotional work. Pencil, mono print, oil pastel, watercolor, Photoshop

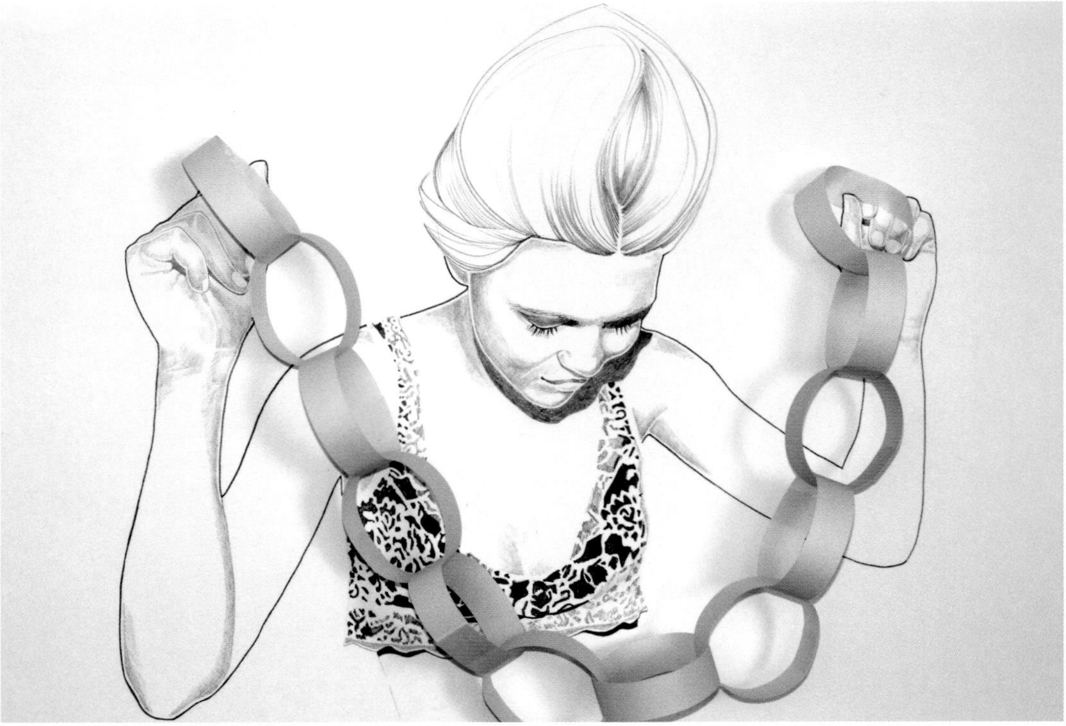

Paper Chains. Personal work. Mixed media, collage

We WouldAll Be Kings. Exhibition piece. Mixed media

Allan o olwg,
allan o feddwl

Out of Sight Out Of Mind. Exhibition piece. Mixed media

Sing to your Grandmother a Sweet Song. Exhibition piece. Mixed media

Fortune Teller. Personal work. Mixed media, collage

Too Much is never enough. Exhibition piece. Ball pen

Smokers. Personal work

Roberta Zeta Italy www.robertazeta.com

Barret. Personal work

A Rose. Personal work

Iggy. Personal work

Marc Jacobs. Die Zeit. Pencil

Stuart whitton UK www.stuartwhitton.co.uk

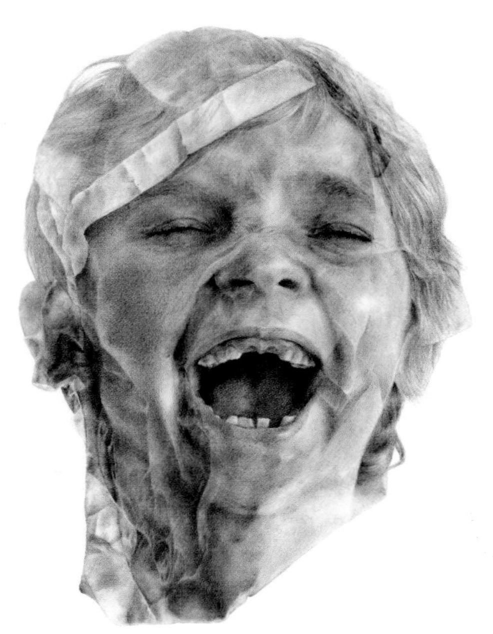

Laughter. Personal work. Pencil

Brother. Personal work. Pencil

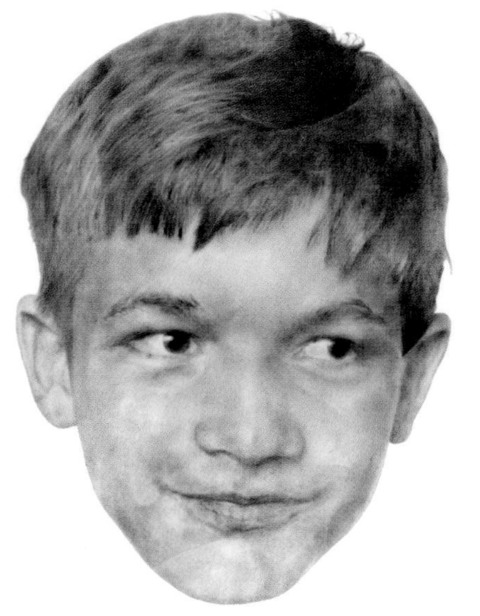

Mischief. Personal work. Pencil

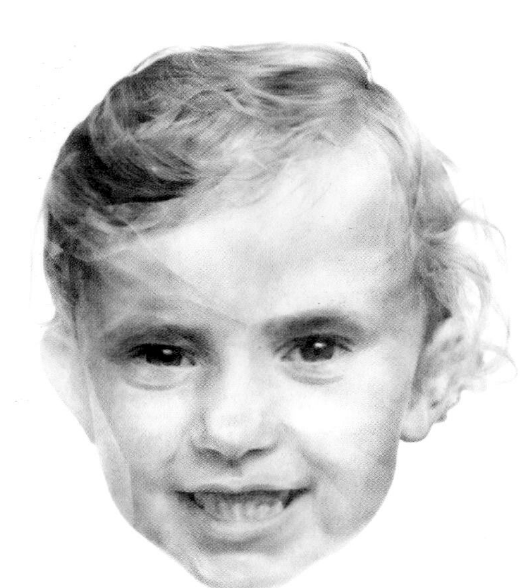

Origin. Personal work. Pencil

Alexis Marcou Greece www.alexismarcou.com

Ms Antiqua. Insanity. Hand drawing and digital

O2. Personal work. Hand drawing and digital

Kyaker. Black Swan Life for Crusoe. Hand drawing and digital

Superherors SF. Society 6. Hand drawing and digital

Biker. Black Swan Life for Crusoe. Hand drawing and digital

Oliver Barrett USA www.ohbarrett.com

Lecter. Scream Prints. Mixed media

I Know you Are. G1988. Graphite, digital

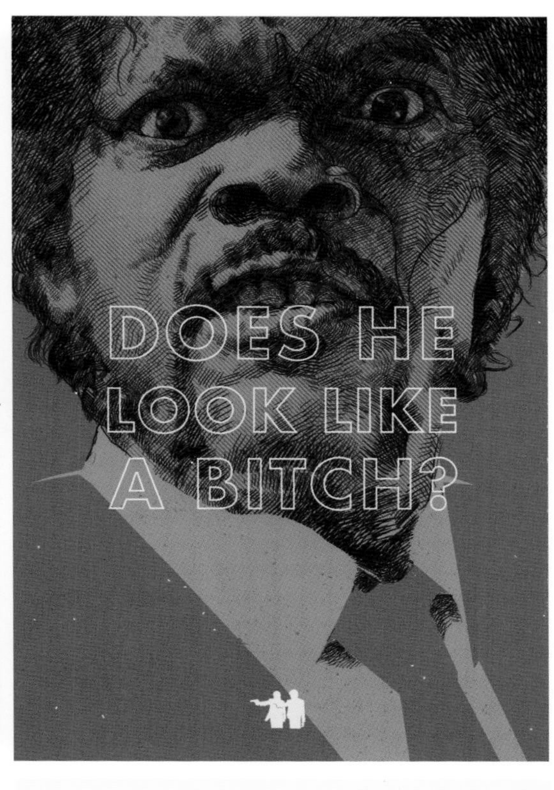

What does Marcellus Wallace Look Like. Spoke Art. Mixed media

Coltrane. Personal work. Mixed media

Mingus. Personal work. Mixed media

Joel Benjamin UK www.joelbenjamin.co.uk

Thom Yorke. Personal work. Indian Ink, watercolor, Photoshop

Fleet Foxes. Personal work. Indian Ink, watercolor, Photoshop

Clint Eastwood. Personal work. Indian Ink, watercolor, Photoshop

Shades. Personal work. Indian Ink, watercolor, Photoshop

Action Fashion. ELLE

Agata Endo Nowicka Poland www.agatanowicka.com

Kuba Wojewodzki, Entertainer. Bluszcz

Zuza Ziomecka. ELLE

Wislawa Szymborska, Poet. GALA

Robert Kusmirowski, Artist. Lampa

Tiffany Antrim as Catwoman. Personal work. Graphite, charcoal on toned paper

Mrs. Ricci. Personal work. Watercolor on paper

Tia. Personal work. Watercolor on paper

Eve. Personal work. Watercolor on paper

Mrs. West-Pinto. Personal work. Watercolor on paper

The Man Behind the Cloud. The Korn/Ferry Institute magazine Briefings on Talent & Leadership. Mixed media

Zé Otavio Brazil www.zeotavio.com

John Lennon, The Early Years. Personal work. Mixed media

Paul, The Early Years. Personal work. Mixed media

Lenine. Rolling Stone Brazil. Mixed media

Julian Assange. O Estado de Sao Paulo. Mixed media

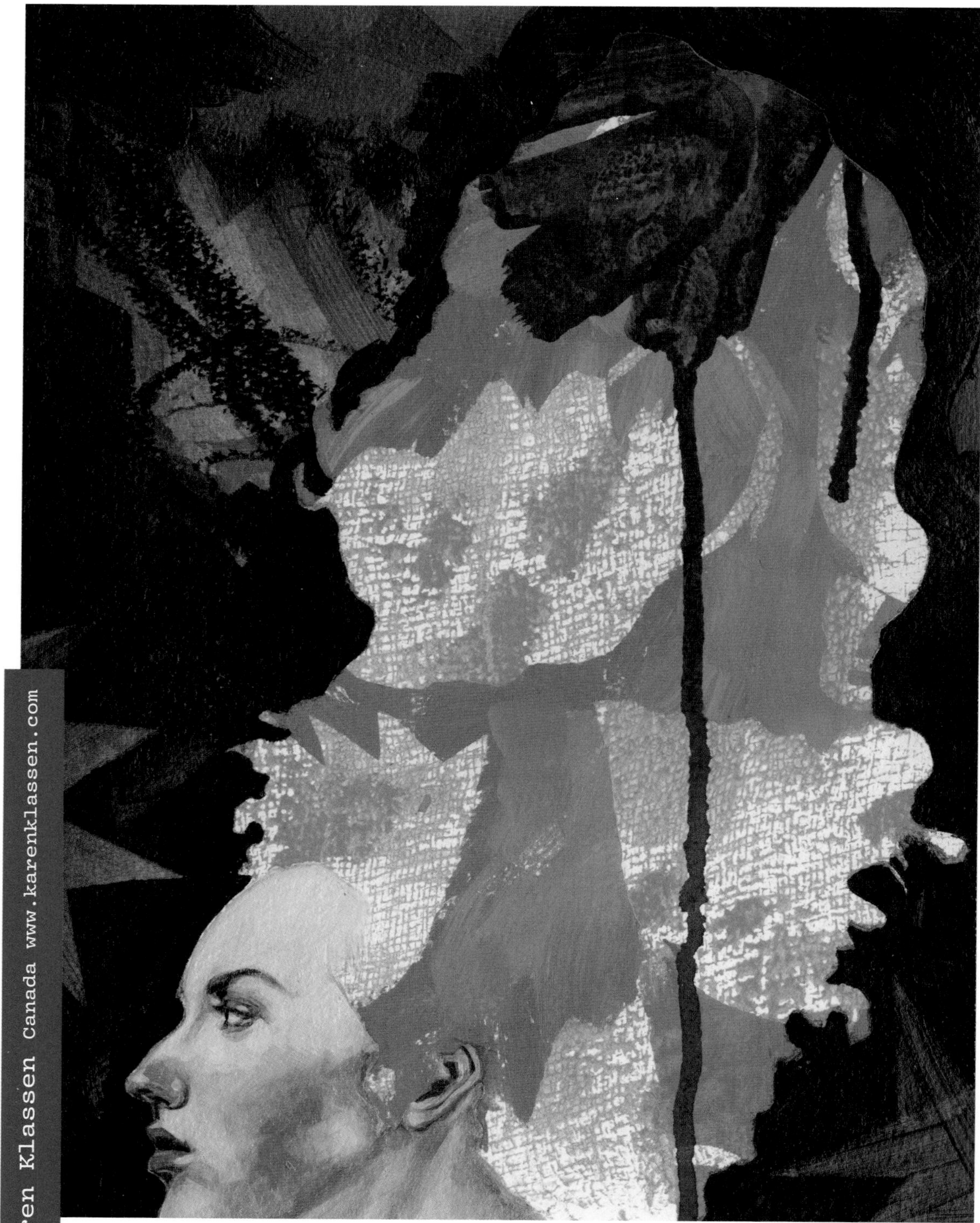

Karen Klassen Canada www.karenklassen.com

Beehive. Personal work. Acrylic, oil stick, oil paint

Lolita Project: Lola. Personal work. Acrylic, oil

Lolita Project: Chris. Personal work. Acrylic, oil

Lolita Project: Jennifer. Personal work. Acrylic, oil

Lolita Project: Amy. Personal work. Acrylic, oil

Randy Glass USA www.randyglassstudio.com

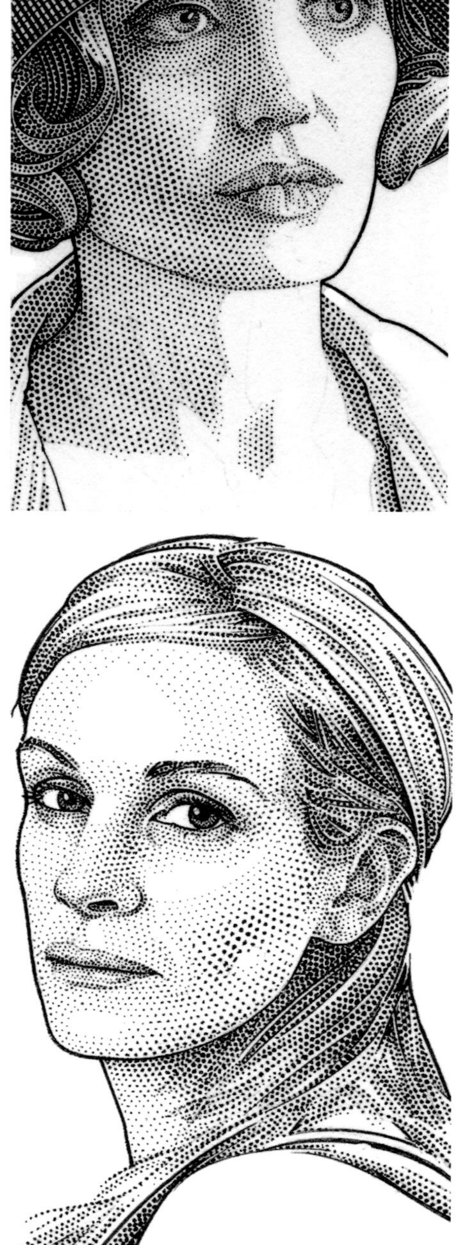

Angelina Jolie. Wall Street Journal. Pen, inc

Julia Roberts. Wall Street Journal. Pen, inc

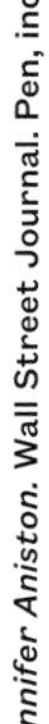

Jennifer Aniston. Wall Street Journal. Pen, inc

Queen Latifah. Wall Street Journal. Pen, inc

Robert Downey Jr. Wall Street Journal. Pen, inc

Sean Penn. Wall Street Journal. Pen, inc

Tom Hanks. Wall Street Journal. Pen, inc

Samuel L. Jackson. Wall Street Journal. Pen, inc

Virgin Girl. Be Magazine. Photoshop, watercolor

Anne Cresci France www.annecresci.com

Scarlett Johansson. Cosmopolitan magazine. Photoshop, watercolor

Keira Knightley. Cosmopolitan magazine. Photoshop, watercolor

Matt Chinn UK www.mattchinn.co.uk

Bearded. Personal work. Digital

Uffie. Personal work. Digital

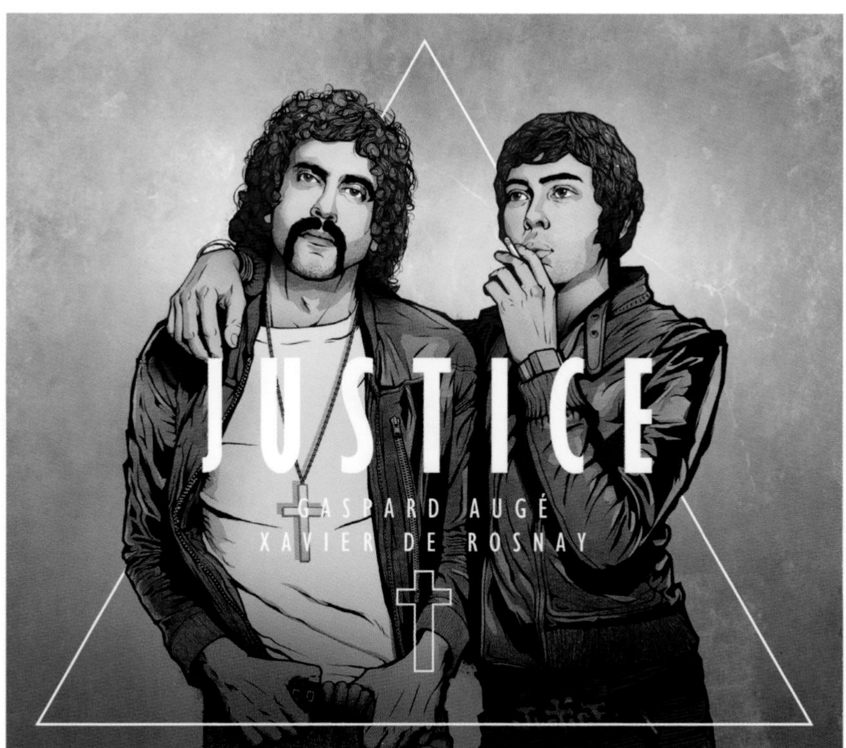

Justice. Personal work. Digital

MEGA BURGER!
CHAMPION